IS BOOK BELONGS TO:

MICHAEL A. BEEBE

GIVEN ON HIS 8ᵗʰ
BIRTHDAY BY:

GRANDPA & GRANDMA
9/16/92   BEEBE

home-built
AIRPLANES

home-built
AIRPLANES

DON BERLINER

Lerner Publications Company ▪ Minneapolis, Minnesota

ACKNOWLEDGMENTS: All of the photographs in this book have been provided by the author.

LIBRARY OF CONGRESS CATALOGING IN PUBLICATION DATA

Berliner, Don.
    Home-built airplanes.

    (Superwheels and Thrill Sports)
    SUMMARY: Discusses the history, design, construction, and testing of amateur-built airplanes.

    1. Airplanes, Home-built — Juvenile literature.
[1. Airplanes, Home-built] I. Title. II. Series.

TL671.2.B455 1979   629.133'343   79-1460
ISBN 0-8225-0433-2

Manufactured in the United States of America.

International Standard Book Number: 0-8225-0433-2
Library of Congress Catalog Card Number: 79-1460

2 3 4 5 6 7 8 9 10 90 89 88 87 86 85 84 83 82 81

CONTENTS

The Experimental Aircraft Association annual fly-in at Oshkosh, Wisconsin

INTRODUCTION

Not all airplanes are built in factories. The world's airports are full of well-made, factory-built Cessna, Piper, and Beech airplanes, but to some people these planes seem too much alike. They are also expensive to buy. Today there are thousands of airplanes being put together in home workshops by people who think that the only way to have an inexpensive and truly individual airplane is to build it. These people are proud of their planes. Every amateur-built airplane has the word "experimental" painted on its side, so everyone will know it was not built in a factory.

Building an airplane doesn't cost a lot of money, but it often takes years of hard work. Skill and patience are required to make the thousands of little parts that must someday fit together and work perfectly. Most people find that building their first airplane takes three or four years, even if they spend all their evenings and weekends on the project.

People build their own airplanes for many different reasons. Some build them because they want to fly but don't have enough money to buy a new airplane or even a used one that is in good condition. For these people, an airplane is mainly a fast way to travel. They build two- or four-seat planes that are meant for fast cruising.

Other people build airplanes because they like to remember the "good old days" when flying was new and seemed to be so much fun. Some of these people build open-cockpit *biplanes* that have two wings on each side of the *fuselage* (body of the plane). The upper and lower wings are connected with wires and braces that make a loud howling sound in flight. Other people build replicas that are exact copies of World War I or World War II fighter planes. Pilots of these planes have the feeling of being one of the glamorous flyers of aviation's early history.

Other people like to build planes called "radicals" that attract a lot of attention wherever they land. These unusual airplanes are experiments in design or materials, but they are often slow, noisy, and not very comfortable. Some have no covering over the fuselage and, as a result, look old even if they are brand new. Others have unusual shapes or new design features that make them different from other planes.

Most racing pilots build their own airplanes. Some design their planes as well, but others use sets of plans designed by someone else that can be purchased by the builder.

A Cassutt sport-racer lands after a successful test flight.

The most popular of these are plans for the Cassutt Racer, a plane that was designed by a former racing champion. Even people who don't plan to race build Cassutts because they are attractive and fast little airplanes.

Many airplanes are specially designed and built for aerobatics. In the past, when this was a very dangerous sport, it was called "stunt flying." Now, stronger planes designed especially for difficult maneuvers in the sky are used, and as a result, the sport is much safer. Most aerobatic airplanes are biplanes, but now some people are designing and building *monoplanes* (planes with a single wing on each side of the fuselage) for this purpose.

THE HISTORY OF HOME-BUILT AIRPLANES

Back in 1903, when the Wright brothers built the first airplane that really worked, they did it for a serious purpose. They had invented a new kind of vehicle. They worked to improve it and to sell airplanes to other people. But soon afterward people started to make their own airplanes at home just for the fun of building and flying them. A few years after Orville Wright made the first successful flight, magazines began to appear that showed people how to build airplanes at home. One plane that was popular with amateur builders of that time was the Blériot. This was a small monoplane like the one in which French aviator Louis Blériot made the first over-water flight. He crossed the English Channel on July 25, 1909, in 37 minutes.

During World War I (1914-1918), many improvements were made in airplane design. Early in the war, Germany, the United States, and other countries began to make swift fighter planes and heavy bombers. At the beginning of W.W. I most planes could fly 60 to 70 miles (97 to 110 kilometers) per hour. By the time the war ended, planes were being made that could go as fast as 130 miles (209 kilometers) per hour.

After the war, the United States government offered thousands of these planes for sale at bargain prices. People could buy the planes and change them in any way they wanted. This increased the popularity of

This 1911 Blériot can still fly in calm weather.

flying, building, and working on airplanes for fun.

By the 1930s thousands of people had become interested in building small airplanes. But in the United States, the government decided that home-built airplanes were unsafe and made them illegal. Then World War II started in 1939, and interest in home-built planes declined. Pilots were flying bombers and fighter planes for their countries, and other people were too busy with the war to give much time to hobbies.

This early home-built airplane has been carefully painted.

When the war ended, people again became interested in building airplanes at home. In 1947 the United States government began allowing airplane building by amateurs but it established rules and safety regulations so that home-built airplanes would be safer than they had been before the war.

In 1953 a group of people who wanted to build airplanes gathered in Milwaukee, Wisconsin, to start a club. They called it the Experimental Aircraft Association, or EAA. A few months after that first meeting, the group held its first "fly-in," an outdoor meeting of people who are interested in airplanes. Most of the airplanes brought to that first meet were factory-made planes that had been modified, or changed, by their owners. For example, a plane's wings might have been shortened or moved from the upper part of the fuselage to the lower. Some of the changes were successful and some were not, but the planes were different from factory-built planes and attracted attention. The EAA began to grow. Local chapters were started in other parts of the United States, in Canada, and in other countries. By 1975 the EAA had 50,000 members and 500 local chapters. More than 5,000 home-built airplanes were flying and over 10,000 were being built. In the United States alone, there were twice as many home-built airplanes flying as there were commercial airliners.

As the Experimental Aircraft Association grew, its fly-in became a bigger event every year. Since 1970 it has been held at the Oshkosh, Wisconsin, airport in late July and early August. It is the world's largest aviation meet, and for one week of the year

Display airplanes in the early-morning mist at the Oshkosh annual fly-in

the Oshkosh airport, Wittman Field, is the world's busiest airport. Altogether, nearly 1,500 airplanes are on display every year, and thousands more bring visitors to the fly-in.

The display airplanes at the fly-in are parked in groups. There are old warplanes, classics (planes built between 1946 and 1955), and antiques (planes built before World War II). There are even little one-person gyrocopters, which are like small helicopters, and a few full-size home-built helicopters. But the biggest display — the reason that thousands of people visit the Oshkosh fly-in every year — is in the center of the field near the main gate. Between 400 and 500 amateur-built airplanes are parked there. They have been flown in from all parts of the United States and Canada. Over a hundred kinds can be seen, and they are of all sizes, shapes, and colors.

Some of these home-built airplanes are brand new designs. They attract the most interest from the EAA members. Each new type is studied carefully to see what is different about it. There may be a new wing design that is supposed to make the plane faster. Or a plane may be made from a new material never used in airplane building. Or different ways of streamlining parts of the airplane may have been tried. Experimental aircraft builders are always looking for new ideas to use in their own workshops.

Other home-built planes are made from standard sets of plans that can be purchased through the Association. Some designs are so popular that there may be 40 or more of each kind in a row. This makes it easy for people who are building that kind of airplane to find the best way of making certain parts. Many people visit the Oshkosh fly-in just to learn how to build their favorite airplanes.

Airplane builders can also attend forums and workshops and visit large buildings where airplane pieces and plans are sold. The forums are meetings with flying and airplane-building experts. The workshops teach the skills of airplane building such as welding and working with metal, wood, fiberglass, and fabric.

As many as 100,000 people come to the Oshkosh fly-in, some from as far away as England, Japan, and Australia. As soon as they get home most people begin making plans to return to Oshkosh the following year.

Visitors examine a display of home-built airplanes at Oshkosh.

POPULAR HOME-BUILT AIRPLANES

A person who wants to build a flying machine can choose from at least 150 different designs. Some are for planes that have been built and flown for many years, while others are new and different. There are designs for biplanes and monoplanes. There are designs for planes that can carry only the pilot and for planes that can carry passengers. In some of these planes the pilot and passenger sit side by side while in others the passenger sits behind the pilot.

designed in 1943 and has been brought up to date with larger engines and a stronger structure. It is the best aerobatic airplane of the home-builts and has one of the best sets of plans. More than 300 of these planes are now flying. The Smith Miniplane was first built and flown in 1965. Since then, more than 100 have been built. The wings of this little plane are made of wood, and the fuselage and tail are made of steel. The entire airplane is covered with fabric.

SINGLE-SEAT BIPLANES

Among the several single-seat biplanes that can be built are the Pitts Special and the Smith Miniplane. The Pitts Special was

TWO-SEAT BIPLANES

People who want to build two-seat biplanes often choose the Starduster Too, which is the most popular of all the open-cockpit two-

The single-seat Pitts Special *(right)* is shorter than the two-seat version of the same plane *(left)*.

wingers. The plans for this plane were developed from the original Starduster, which was smaller and less complicated to build, but which used the same materials and skills.

The Steen Skybolt is also a popular two-seat biplane. It was designed in 1968 and is one of the best aerobatic airplanes with two seats.

This Smith Miniplane, built by Connie Marsh, is a colorful example of a popular design.

The Starduster Too is a two-seat biplane that amateurs often choose to build.

The design of the Steen Skybolt is also popular among amateur builders.

The Volksplane (*above*) is an all-wood plane with a boxlike design. The outside of the Bowers Fly Baby shown here (*right*) has been painted to resemble planks of wood.

ALL-WOOD MONOPLANES

The Evans VP-1 (Volksplane) and the Bowers Fly Baby are two all-wood monoplanes that are popular with home builders. The Volksplane with its Volkswagen engine is simple to build and easy to fly. A variation of the Volksplane design, the VP-2, carries two people and uses a slightly larger VW engine. The designer of the Bowers Fly Baby, Pete Bowers, won an EAA Design Competition prize with his one-person airplane. It has a wood-covered fuselage and fabric-covered wings. There will soon be more than 700 of these popular planes built and flying.

The sleek design of the Midget Mustang shows that it was built for racing.

The Thorp T-18 was the first home-built airplane to fly around the world.

ALL-METAL MONOPLANES

The Midget Mustang and the Thorp T-18 are two all-metal monoplanes that are often built by amateurs. The Midget Mustang, a one-seat airplane, was first built in 1947 as a racing plane. A two-seat version is called the Mustang II. The Thorp T-18 is a side-by-side cabin airplane and was first flown in 1964. More than 150 of these have been built since then; in 1976 the T-18 became the first home-built airplane to fly around the world.

23

This red Wittman Tailwind is a well-designed and well-known monoplane.

The Stits Skycoupe is one of the earliest EAA designs. This Skycoupe is named *Black Magic*.

WOOD, METAL, AND FABRIC MONOPLANES

There are many designs for monoplanes made of a combination of wood, metal, and fabric. Two of the most popular are the Tailwind and the Skycoupe. The Wittman Tailwind is a high-winged airplane in which two people sit next to each other in a closed cabin. It was designed in 1952 by Steve Wittman, the most famous of all racing plane builders. More than 100 of these planes are flying. In addition to the home-builts, a few have been made by a small factory in England. The Stits Skycoupe is one of the earliest EAA airplanes. It carries two people in a very strong airframe (fuselage, wings, and tail). The Skycoupe is not a very fast airplane, but it is popular because it can take off from small airfields easily.

FOAM AND FIBERGLASS AIRPLANES

Airplanes made of foam and fiberglass are a relatively new development in airplane building. The Rutan VariEze is the first of the really modern light airplanes. Its name suggests the words "very easy" because it can be built relatively quickly. Its thin wings are at the back of the fuselage, and have little winglets on the tips to make the plane fly better. The tail assembly, which is in the rear of most planes, is in front of this airplane. The first VariEze was built in 10 weeks and soon set a record by flying more than 1,600 miles without stopping. Most of its parts are made of blocks of plastic foam covered with layers of fiberglass cloth that make the plane very strong and light. It is an economical plane that can fly up to 30 miles per gallon of gas.

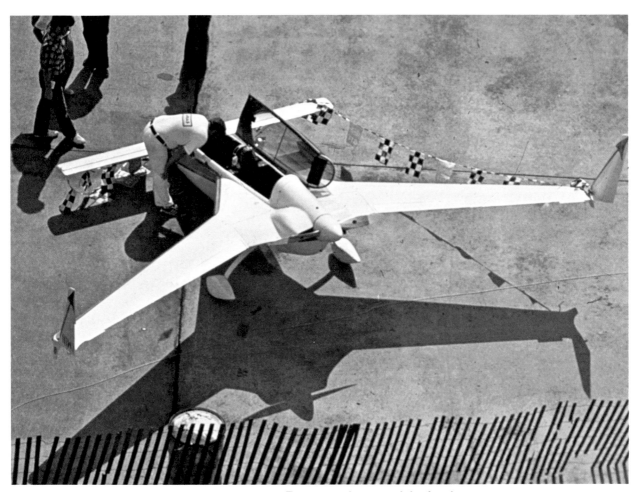

The wings of the VariEze are at the rear of the fuselage.

The Quicky has an unusual design. Its wheels are in the tips of the front wings, and another set of wings is just behind the pilot's seat.

The Quicky is the smallest airplane that can be built from plans. It has one wing on each side of the nose and another just behind the pilot's seat. The wheels are in the tips of the front wings. This is an economical plane because it will get 100 miles per gallon of gas.

REPLICAS

Many people like to build replicas of famous airplanes such as military planes from World War I and World War II. Plans for smaller versions of these planes are available. One of the most popular is the Fokker D.R. 1 Triplane, the three-winged plane that the German flying ace, the "Red Baron" von Richthofen, made famous. Replicas of this plane are usually painted bright red. Some builders include mock machine guns that fire blanks so that they can have make-believe air battles with other replicas.

Another popular replica is the P-51 Mustang. This famous W.W. II fighter plane can be built of wood in one-half, two-thirds, or three-fourths the size of the original. When they are painted like military airplanes, these scale Mustangs look much like the real thing. The Corsair, Spitfire, and Focke Wulf 190 are other fighter planes that can be built in smaller-scale versions.

Replicas of the World War I Fokker Triplane, made famous by the Red Baron, are popular with airplane builders who are interested in history.

This P-51 Mustang, built at two-thirds the original size, is a good replica of the famous World War II fighter planes.

A pilot who flies the Breezy must hope for good weather.

RADICALS

Plans can also be obtained for home-built airplanes of unusual design. These planes are called "radicals" because their designs are so different from traditional airplane styles. One of them, for example, the Breezy, has wings from an old Piper Super Cruiser, a backwards-mounted engine, and no covering on the fuselage. It is meant for flying in good weather only, because the pilot and passenger sit out in the open like people riding a tandem bicycle.

The wings of John Dyke's Delta are shaped like a triangle, or the Greek letter *delta*. This streamlined aircraft will carry four people in a comfortable cabin. It is the only delta-winged airplane that will fly well at low speed. Other deltas are fast jets.

The Flying Flea is a funny old design that has been brought up to date and made completely safe. It was first built in the 1930s by a man who couldn't learn to fly an ordinary airplane. Because of this he made some serious mistakes in the design, and several pilots were killed before the plane was made safe. Now it is one of the easiest airplanes to fly. It can take off and land on small airstrips. It can be built in many sizes, with engines of 25 to 100 horsepower. The "Flea" is not a fast plane, but it is popular because people enjoy building it.

The Delta is a comfortable passenger aircraft.

This is an early Flying Flea, built around 1936.

BUILDING YOUR OWN AIRPLANE

Building a real airplane is not quite as easy as building a model airplane. A home-built aircraft has to carry in it at least one human being, and that means it has to be built with special care. It must be inspected many times by its builder and, if it is built in the United States, at least three times by the U.S. Federal Aviation Agency (FAA). A home-built airplane is also more complicated and takes much longer to build than a model plane. But since building is a large part of the fun of this hobby, the length of time it takes usually isn't important. Many men and women work on one airplane for years and then sell it soon after it has flown for the first time. Once a builder has some experience building one plane, he or she can probably build a second plane in about half the time.

CHOOSING A DESIGN

If you plan to build an airplane, first you must decide which design is right for you. The best way to do this is to talk to people who have built different kinds of airplanes. They can tell you about their experiences and can show you which planes are as good as they look and which are hard to build or hard to fly.

You can also go to fly-ins and look carefully at some examples of airplanes you find interesting. If, for instance, you want to build an open-cockpit biplane that carries only the pilot, you have quite a wide choice of plans. You can talk to people at the fly-in who have built airplanes of this kind, and you can see for yourself what they are really like.

A person who decides to build an airplane must spend many hours in a workshop. This well-equipped workshop belongs to a builder in England.

Once you have decided which airplane you want to build, you must buy a set of plans. They cost from $25 to $100, depending on the design. Plans can be as simple as a few pages of paper, or as complete as 50 or more large sheets of drawings. Some plans show you how to build just the main parts of the airplane and let you figure out how to build the rest. Others show you every little piece drawn with great care. How quickly you build your plane depends upon how well you can read blueprints and how much mechanical work you have done before.

When you have the plans, it is important to study them carefully so that you can remember almost every line and measurement. You should know exactly the order in which the parts are built. If something is done out of order, it may have to be torn up and started over.

PUTTING THE PIECES TOGETHER

Most people build the fuselage of the airplane first. The fuselages of small airplanes are usually built from slim pipes or tubing of a fine steel called "chrome-moly." Pieces of this steel must be cut carefully with a special saw and then fitted together on a large table. A drawing of the side of the fuselage is made right on the table top so that the builder can see exactly where each piece goes. The tubing is then welded together by the builder or by an expert welder if the builder is a beginner. When both sides of the fuselage have been made, they are propped up and cross-pieces of tubing are welded between them. This creates a long box of steel tubes. To make it easier to move the completed fuselage around, the landing gear and wheels are often built next and attached.

The most difficult single part of the airplane to build is the wings. They are usually made from many curved *ribs* or strips of wood. The ribs are either sawed out of large sheets of plywood or built up from small

Metal tubing is welded together to form the fuselage.

pieces of spruce or plywood. They are then glued to a long thick piece of spruce, the *spar*, which runs all the way from one wingtip to the other. Most wings are then covered with aircraft cloth, but some are covered with thin sheets of plywood.

The wings are attached to the fuselage with strong bolts that pass through heavy steel plates. This makes sure that the wings do not break off when the airplane flies through bumpy air or when it makes sharp turns. The tail parts, sometimes called the "tail feathers," are made from short pieces of steel tubing or, occasionally, wood. They are also connected to the fuselage with bolts and plates.

When you have built the main parts of the airplane, it is time to attach the engine. Most home-built planes use regular small airplane engines that are purchased already made. Others use modified automobile engines such as the four-cylinder Volkswagen. The engine must be carefully bolted to the front of the airplane, and its controls and instruments must be hooked up and tested.

Before any parts of the airplane can be covered, an inspector from the Federal Aviation Agency must look at the plane carefully to make sure everything has been built right. The inspector will look at each place where two parts are glued, welded, or bolted together. He or she will thump, wiggle, and shake every part of the airplane to make sure nothing is loose. The FAA inspector may seem to you to be very suspicious, but the careful inspection is really in the builder's interest because it makes sure the airplane will be as safe as possible.

An engine is attached to a partly finished Wittman Tailwind.

After this first official inspection, it is time to cover the airplane's frame, paint it, and then test the engine. When all this has been done and you are satisfied with your work, the FAA inspector will again examine the plane before you are issued a license for a test flight. With that license, as well as a pilot's license, you can take your airplane to an airport for testing.

THE FIRST TEST FLIGHT

At the airport, you must first taxi up and down the runway to see how your plane handles on the ground. If it steers and tracks satisfactorily, it is time to fly the plane. This is always very exciting for the builder. You

A builder covers an airplane frame, cutting and shaping pieces of foam to an exact fit. Next, she will cover the foam with fiberglass cloth.

have worked for thousands of hours to make this aircraft, and now you will know how well it can fly.

It is best to make the first test flight early in the morning or in the evening, when the air is calm. Before you start, you must check every part of the airplane that you can see — the control surfaces on the wings (the flaps and ailerons) and tail (the rudder and elevator), the engine, the propellor, the landing gear, and all the places where one part of the plane is attached to another. You then climb into your airplane and hook up your seat belt and shoulder harness. You start the engine and let it warm up. When the needles on the engine instruments point to their green, or ready-to-fly, areas, you can begin the take-off.

You taxi out to the end of the runway and look around to make sure that no other airplanes are trying to land or take off. Your plane, like most home-builts, does not have a radio so you must be on the alert for other planes at all times. Air traffic can come from any direction, even above or below when you are in flight.

As soon as all is clear, you push the throttle all the way forward and start down the runway. As your airplane picks up speed, you feel the controls starting to work. The wheels skip lightly across the runway and then leave the ground. You are in the air! An airplane you have built with your own hands is flying, just as the Wright brothers' first airplane did more than 75 years ago. You sail along with only the sounds of your engine and

The tank of a Cassutt sport-racer is filled before its first flight.

the wind in your ears. You have achieved a great victory.

After one or two laps around the traffic pattern, it is time to land. You line up with the runway and cut back on the engine's power. Your airplane settles gently onto the runway and quickly slows down so that you can turn toward the hangar. There your friends are waiting to congratulate you. This is an important occasion, and they may even cut off part of your shirt tail with a pair of scissors—a tradition among people who build airplanes.

After that first flight you check your airplane from propellor to tail feathers to make sure nothing has come loose. If the airplane didn't fly exactly the way you wanted it to, you will make the necessary changes before the next flight.

After about 40 hours of test-flying near your home airport, you will ask the FAA inspector to examine your plane once again. When the inspector is satisfied you will be given a license that allows you to fly the plane anywhere you want to, within the limits of safety. If your airplane has more than one seat, you can now carry passengers. When your plane has that second license, you have come to the end of a long and sometimes difficult process. You have put in thousands of hours of planning, work, and testing. The satisfaction you feel gives you a sense of accomplishment that makes you proud of what you know and have done.

SPECIFICATIONS OF SOME HOME-BUILT AIRPLANES

	LENGTH		WING SPAN		ENGINE HORSEPOWER	CRUISING SPEED	EMPTY WEIGHT	
Single-Seat Biplanes								
Pitts Special	15	ft.	17.5	ft.	180	140 mph	750	lb.
	4.5	m	5.25	m		224 kph	337.5	kg
Smith Miniplane	15	ft.	15.75	ft. (lower)	125	120 mph	650	lb.
	4.5	m	4.725	m		192 kph	292.5	kg
			17	ft. (upper)				
			5.1	m				
Two-Seat Biplanes								
Starduster Too	20	ft.	24	ft.	180	120 mph	1,100	lb.
	6	m	7.2	m		192 kph	495	kg
Steen Skybolt	19	ft.	23	ft.	180	120 mph	1,100	lb.
	5.7	m	6.9	m		192 kph	495	kg
All-Wood Monoplanes								
Evans VP-1	18	ft.	24	ft.	40	75 mph	450	lb.
(Volksplane)	5.4	m	7.2	m		120 kph	202.5	kg
Bowers Fly Baby	18.5	ft.	28	ft.	85	100 mph	600	lb.
	5.55	m	8.4	m		160 kph	270	kg
All-Metal Monoplanes								
Midget Mustang	16.5	ft.	18.5	ft.	85	150 mph	575	lb.
	4.8	m	5.55	m		240 kph	258.15	kg

	LENGTH		WING SPAN		ENGINE HORSEPOWER	CRUISING SPEED	EMPTY WEIGHT	
All-Metal Monoplanes								
Thorp T-18	18	ft.	21	ft.	180	175 mph	900	lb.
	5.4	m	6.3	m		280 kph	405	kg
Wood, Metal, and Fabric Monoplanes								
Wittman Tailwind	20	ft.	22.5	ft.	100	160 mph	800	lb.
	6	m	6.75	m		256 kph	360	kg
Stits Skycoupe	19	ft.	27	ft.	65	95 mph	650	lb.
	5.7	m	8.1	m		152 kph	292.5	kg
Foam and Fiberglass Airplanes								
Rutan VariEze	14	ft.	22	ft.	100	200 mph	535	lb.
	4.2	m	6.6	m		320 kph	240.75	kg
Quicky	17.33	ft.	16	ft.	18	120 mph	240	lb.
	5.2	m	4.8	m		192 kph	108	kg
Replicas								
Fokker D.R. 1 Triplane	19	ft.	17, 18, 24	ft.	150	100 mph	1,500	lb.
	5.7	m	5.1, 5.4, 7.2	m		160 kph	675	kg
P-51 Mustang (¾ size)	21.5	ft.	24.69	ft.	200	150 mph	1,485	lb.
	6.45	m	7.4	m		240 kph	668.25	kg
Radicals								
Breezy	22.5	ft.	33	ft.	90	75 mph	700	lb.
	6.75	m	9.9	m		120 kph	315	kg
Dyke Delta	19	ft.	22	ft.	180	180 mph	950	lb.
	5.7	m	6.6	m		288 kph	427.5	kg

Superwheels & Thrill Sports

Airplanes
AEROBATICS
AIRPLANE RACING
HELICOPTERS
HOME-BUILT AIRPLANES
PERSONAL AIRPLANES
THE WORLD'S GREATEST AIRPLANES: I & II
YESTERDAY'S AIRPLANES

Automobiles & Auto Racing
AMERICAN RACE CAR DRIVERS
THE DAYTONA 500
DRAG RACING
ICE RACING
THE INDIANAPOLIS 500
INTERNATIONAL RACE CAR DRIVERS
LAND SPEED RECORD BREAKERS
RALLYING
ROAD RACING
TRACK RACING

CLASSIC SPORTS CARS
DINOSAUR CARS: LATE GREAT CARS
   FROM 1945 TO 1966

FABULOUS CARS OF THE 1920s & 1930s
KIT CARS: CARS YOU CAN BUILD YOURSELF
MODEL CARS
RESTORING OLD CARS
VANS: THE PERSONALITY VEHICLES
YESTERDAY'S CARS

Bicycles
BICYCLE ROAD RACING
BICYCLE TRACK RACING
BICYCLES ON PARADE

Motorcycles
GRAND NATIONAL CHAMPIONSHIP RACES
MOPEDS: THE GO-EVERYWHERE BIKES
MOTOCROSS MOTORCYCLE RACING
MOTORCYCLE RACING
MOTORCYCLES ON THE MOVE
THE WORLD'S BIGGEST MOTORCYCLE RACE:
   THE DAYTONA 200
YESTERDAY'S MOTORCYCLES

Other Specialities
KARTING
SAILBOAT RACING
SKYDIVING
SNOWMOBILE RACING
YESTERDAY'S FIRE ENGINES
YESTERDAY'S TRAINS

Lerner Publications Company
241 First Avenue North, Minneapolis, Minnesota 55401